JUAN MONTOYA

JUAN MONTOYA

WRITTEN BY ELIZABETH GAYNOR

THE MONACELLI PRESS

Copyright © 2009 The Monacelli Press, a division of Random House, Inc.

All rights reserved.

Published in the United States by The Monacelli Press,
a division of Random House, Inc.
1745 Broadway, New York, New York 10019

The Monacelli Press and colophon are trademarks of Random House, Inc.

Library of Congress Control Number: 2009925118
ISBN: 978-1-58093-244-8

Printed in Italy

10 9 8 7 6 5 4 3 2 1
First edition

Project Editor: Karen Lehrman Bloch/Grafia Books
Design by Matsumoto Incorporated, New York

www.monacellipress.com

Photo Credits: Giorgio Baroni: 261, 263–68; Gordon Beall/*Architectural Digest* © Condé Nast Publications: 127, 129–41; Walter Briski Jr.: 2; Billy Cunningham: 25, 32, 93, 95–103, 287, 289–301; Cunningham/*Architectural Digest* © Condé Nast Publications: 105, 107–12, 114–15; Pieter Estersohn: 183, 185, 186, 188–90; Marina Faust: 203, 205–10, 212–17, 219, 221, 222–23, 225, 226; Scott Frances: 35, 37, 38, 40–43, 45, 46, 48–51, 53, 229, 231–33, 235, 236, 238–41, 243, 271, 273–78, 281–83, 285; John M. Hall/*Architectural Digest* © Condé Nast Publications: 143, 145, 146–47, 149, 150, 152–57; Ken Hayden: 65, 67–77, 117, 119–25; Eric Laignel: cover, 9, 11, 12–16, 18–23, 55, 57–63, 79, 81–86, 88–90; Michael Moran: 171, 173–75, 177, 178, 181, 245, 247–49, 251–57, 259; Eric Piasecki: 27–31, 159, 161–69; Durston Saylor/*Architectural Digest* © Condé Nast Publications: 193, 195–201

TABLE OF CONTENTS

6
Introduction

8
Beach and Golf Club, Miromar Lakes, Florida

24
Kips Bay Show House, New York City

34
Skylight Apartment, New York City

54
International Design Center, Estero, Florida

64
Beach House, Golden Beach, Florida

78
Rue Jacob Pied-à-Terre, Paris

92
Upper East Side Residence, New York City

104
Park Avenue Apartment, New York City

116
South Beach Flat, Miami Beach, Florida

126
Beach House, Punta Cana, Dominican Republic

142
Country House, Roxbury, Connecticut

158
Madison Avenue Apartment, New York City

170
Villa Maria Show House, Water Mill, Long Island

182
Pool House, Garrison, New York

192
Upstate New York Residence, Pound Ridge, New York

202
Penthouse Duplex, Paris

218
L'Étoile Office, Paris

228
Upper East Side Townhouse, New York City

244
Oceanfront Apartment, Bal Harbour, Florida

260
Harbor View Apartment, Miami Beach, Florida

270
Luxury Tower, Philadelphia, Pennsylvania

286
Fifth Avenue Residence, New York City

303
Acknowledgments

INTRODUCTION

"Give me your dreams and I will make them happen." That's how I like to start a dialogue with my clients—unencumbered by limitations. My role as interior designer is to allow their imagination free rein and then, through the alchemy of architectural gesture, interior know-how, and custom design, fashion a place in which they will be delighted to live . . . or work.

The book you are holding is my second. It gives me great pleasure to present many of the design projects I have completed over the last decade. I've been at this work for thirty years. I love it and I live it in a very personal way, as you'll see, because my own homes are included in these pages. The projects here showcase the wide scope of my work: unique apartments in Paris, relaxed getaways in the tropics, luxurious urban dwellings in Manhattan, rustic homes in rural settings, and more. Along with private dwellings, there are two designer show houses, a beach club, and an international design center.

I don't make any distinction between residential and commercial work in terms of my aesthetic. And that's what makes them equally exciting. I have had the opportunity to design some of the projects featured here from the ground up, to my great satisfaction. I always see things in a three-dimensional, volumetric way, even when I'm sketching the redesign of a single room. I never accept what I see before me as a given: I take it as a canvas.

When I first set up my business many years ago, I was working out of a charming one-bedroom apartment on Sutton Place. I devised an arrangement using the headboard of my bed as a room divider, with the desk and office on the other side. *Interior Design* magazine photographed and wrote about it. The phone started ringing. First I had one employee, then I had two, then I had to move. Interestingly, one of my longtime clients, whose loft-type apartment is in this book, remembered that home office solution and asked me to adapt it to her bedroom.

My work is a product of the architectural training I received in my home country, Colombia, before I emigrated to the States, and of the excellent education I got at the Parsons School of Design in New York, during an especially exciting period. I was taught by dynamic design historians and others who had studied with architectural titans like Louis Kahn. Factor in what I learned post-graduation from a stint at an interior design firm in Paris and another sojourn at a furniture manufacturer in Italy, in combination with the legacy of my Latin roots, and my work began to take on the international flavor that characterizes it today.

I am fascinated by geometry. Consider a triangle, a cube, a rectangle, a circle: they are perfect forms—and a crucial part of my creative process. I can start the sketch for a room by drawing a circle. I ask, "What can this circle do for the space? How do I place the cubes and the triangles to transform it?" And then I begin to look through the shapes deeper into the area. I imagine the focal points. My goal is to create a palpable axis, a clear beacon to create harmony.

The experience of arrival is paramount, so I pay great attention to foyers and entry corridors. I like to invoke curiosity, coupled with a sense of preparation for what lies beyond. I manipulate elegant materials, often with a linear dimension, to create expectation and to suggest the pathway in. I often propose open living plans and like to contrast them with the well-defined entry. With walls or without, there must always be a connection between adjoining spaces. Everything should unfold.

Clients sometimes have an idea of what they want and know their taste, but they rely on a designer for his understanding of scale. Proportion is of utmost importance. Art and furnishings must be sized to make an impact, and large format pieces even enhance a small space. Scale is also an organizing principle, helping to structure the clean, uncluttered spaces I favor. Composition and texture are also influential—as meaningful to me as color. In fact, you'll see that I often work primarily in neutrals so that shapes and movement within the overall composition stand out. I like to use the elements in a room to create rhythm, variations in a fine symphony.

One of the advantages of reaching this juncture in my career is that I have little fear of making mistakes. I invite challenge: a new and complicated project motivates me to contrive an ingenious solution. I can work in myriad decorative styles and enjoy mixing antiques with contemporary pieces. For period rooms I defer to others. I grew up with Louis XV and XVI but now use them selectively, to create an intriguing aesthetic tension.

In the end, I am a tailor for my clients and strive to give them a place that is a good fit. Imposing a particular look on people holds no interest for me. I have clients for whom I first designed a Park Avenue apartment when they were in their early thirties and their young children were a major part of their lives. After a lapse of fifteen years or so, they contacted me again and said, "Well, now that we are getting older, we want it younger." I feel the same about my work—and I was pleased to oblige.

BEACH AND GOLF CLUB, MIROMAR LAKES, FLORIDA, 2007

At the heart of this Florida resort community lies a cluster of deep, man-made lakes, the area chosen for the community's beach and golf club. As artistic director, I collaborated with the architect and design team and bowed deeply to the setting. Using Mediterranean motifs as our template, we deployed a palette of bright whites and naturals to evoke freshness and easy luxury.

A series of arches and fountains leads the visitor to the beach clubhouse, building a sense of anticipation and discovery. For the main entrance, the owner of the resort wanted me to reinterpret ironwork doors she had seen in Europe. I designed an arched gate in a lacy arboreal pattern that both pleases the eye and invites it in, toward a more massive limestone arch across the room inside, establishing a strong sense of visual perspective.

Overall, I wanted to imbue this commercial project with the feeling of a relaxed home. The main seating area is a wide, uncrowded space, a place one can agreeably pass through on the way to another room, or linger in and chat with friends. Doric columns are used to define bays, and the seating groups are straightforward and symmetrical. The stately elements contrast with touches of informality, such as the sisal rugs and the utterly modern, handblown Italian chandelier that is suspended from a mirrored panel, like a shower of teardrops. The library is even more homey, with its matched comfy sofas, traditional curtain treatment, and chimney made of local fieldstone, crossed by a naive wooden mantel.

The two dining areas take their cues from the lakes and the Florida sun. A sweeping curve of windows along one wall of the indoor area ushers in the brilliant blues from outdoors, reflected in a polished wooden floor. The ceiling is a high dome, pierced by arched clerestory windows reminiscent of Romanesque architecture. Unmatched chairs—brown basket-weave leather, blue teal wing chairs, and white upholstered dining chairs—add visual interest. Outside, in the terrace dining area, I allowed nature to set the romantic mood as guests sip glasses of wine. A ficus tree stands as a centerpiece, sending out a tangle of air roots and acting as a natural canopy over the tables. The curlicue ironwork gate here recalls the front entryway, as does the iron furniture, while lanterns and uplighting around the tree enhance the bosky theme.

Previous page: In the entrance hall, the limestone arch and brass and parchment fixtures set a cool Mediterranean tone.

Right: The black iron arboreal entrance gate to the club was designed to echo the natural beauty beyond.

In the main seating area, lounge chairs of my design invite guests to relax and enjoy the view outside. A sisal rug with a two-inch leather border frames the setting.

14

Across the divide, Doric columns elegantly elevate white upholstered furniture and a leather table by Ralph Lauren. The bright whites and neutrals inspire a mood of easy luxury.

A custom handblown glass chandelier from Italy, suspended from a mirrored panel, creates a cascade of different sized amber teardrops over the main seating area.

The perfect symmetry of the library enhances a feeling of elegant comfort. The bronze custom chandelier plays off the stone fireplace, while custom drapes from Holland & Sherry enliven custom sofas and a coffee table by Ralph Lauren.

In the dining room, the high dome ceiling and wraparound view of the lake offer guests a near-spiritual dining experience. The whimsical porcelain chandelier and unmatched chairs add a touch of glamour.

In the terrace dining area, guests can relax in cushioned iron furniture under the shade of a ficus tree. The sound of gentle waves from the lake nearby adds to the tranquility.

KIPS BAY SHOW HOUSE, NEW YORK CITY, 2009

It looked like a room in mourning. That was my initial impression of the large space that ran the full width of a neo-Renaissance townhouse on the Upper East Side, built in the 1920s by the Beaux-Arts schooled architect Charles Pierrepont Henry Gilbert. He had been entrusted to design a dignified home for a prominent merchant, Julius Forstmann, on what was formerly a portion of the Lenox family farm, now a block from Central Park. The enclosure's plentiful woodwork was weighed down with a deep umber stain, giving the room an air of severity.

The old Forstmann mansion had been appropriated by the venerable Kips Bay Boys & Girls Club for its annual decorator show house, and I had been invited to participate. In spite of its superficial handicap, I immediately took to this drawing room, sensing that the three pairs of south-facing French doors spaced symmetrically across the rear wall held the key to its transformation: The rather dour space could be made into an appealing contemporary receiving room by drenching it with light.

I started by painting all of the woodwork—door surrounds, deep moldings, chair-rail-high paneling, and pilasters—as well as the hand-carved quatrefoil ceiling, snow white. Between chair rails and crown moldings, the walls were treated to a combed Venetian plaster technique, giving them a ridged texture paralleling that of the applied columns that flank the fireplace. The delicate ice-toned finish of the combed walls is picked up in the luster of the dusty blue velvet fabric on the major upholstery—the deeply tufted 16-foot banquette that runs along one wall as well as a pair of chaises that establish secondary seating across the room.

"Nordic Light" seemed apt for the room's name. I reinforced the concept with a selection of Swedish antiques, ranging from an elongated, painted table that centers the space, to two exquisite gilded consoles placed on the fireplace wall, to a delightfully idiosyncratic early twentieth-century bedroom set finished in palest celadon and white, which I broke up and sprinkled about. Playing off the delicate tracery of the ceiling's plasterwork is a chandelier of concentric circles and cones, its precise geometry countered by its soft rusty surface.

Filmy linen curtains with deep, tailored headers create translucency along the wall of French doors. Sculpture mounted on white pedestals there becomes ethereal, bathed in daylight. I positioned solid contemporary furniture around the perimeter of the room to anchor the decor, while occasional antique pieces that are lighter in scale and often touched with gilt hew to the luminous theme.

Previous page: A sculpture by Swedish artist Eva Hild rests on a pedestal of my design, both embellished by the room's natural light.

Right: An eighteenth-century Swedish table with a marble top and a metal chandelier of my design mesh with the white walls and woodwork. A metal bench by Ingrid Donat and a leg sculpture by Spanish artist Xavier Mascaró add further textural interest.

The Nordic influence continues: In this corner, two painted Swedish chairs from a 1920s bedroom set, a late-eighteenth-century Swedish gilded console table, and a glass sculpture by Swedish artist Edvin Öhrström set the tableau for a tufted daybed of my design and a stool by John Dickinson. The walls are finished in combed plaster with a silver-pearl veneer.

A buoyant color field painting of mine draws the eye toward this wall, where my 16-foot sectional sofa with white bun feet resides, flanked by Swedish side tables from the 1920s. A cerused oak coffee table of my design provides counterweight.

In this corner, a chair by French designer Christian Badin is accompanied by a French ceramic lamp, a photo of Salvador Dalí by Willy Rizzo, and artwork by Peter Clark.

SKYLIGHT APARTMENT, NEW YORK CITY, 2007

There are a finite number of lofty dwellings in New York City where the skyline is visible from more than one angle. When my clients showed me around the side-by-side apartments they had purchased in a stunning new tower on Manhattan's horizon, I begged them to drop all their preconceptions about how to configure the joined spaces and allow me to make sense of the whole. I felt so strongly about the potential of the generous square footage and the spectacular views that I was willing to do a complete set of plans and redo them if the couple wasn't persuaded.

My idea was to let the main rooms stand virtually open in order to underscore the unobstructed view. I also imagined a foyer and hallway that would visually foreshadow the architectural themes —such as sleek floors and high-polish walls, acting as a splendid showcase for the clients' collections—which I would develop in the rest of the interior.

Corridors can deliberately channel the eye toward specific vantage points, and in a place of this size I was able to create just such an effect. The majestic foyer and gently curving hall lure the visitor into the long living space where seating areas, a dining room, and a den open onto each other. The "rooms" are defined largely by furniture arrangement. All the walls are paneled in mirror finish afromosia wood, and the floor surface is likewise uninterrupted, laid in marble with borders of onyx. My aim was to emphasize continuity, to enhance flow.

The architecture is the star here. I detailed this place meticulously to give character and dignity to a brand-new building and to smooth the transitions between the functional living areas. I wrapped structural columns in fine woodwork and commissioned bas-relief panels as headers for the window walls in the main rooms. I designed several variations of ceiling ornamentation, including elaborate coves that add dimension, and lighting fashioned from precious materials. Most of the wood-clad surfaces are inlaid with bronze, forming a Greek key pattern on some of the doors, dividing long expanses of wall paneling into pleasing modules, and adding the glint of metal to the luster of the lacquered wood throughout.

To balance the abundance of wood and marble, I introduced softness through sumptuous upholstery fabrics, selective use of area rugs, and translucent window wraps—all of which play off each other in a range of warm neutrals. When open, panels of sheer curtains form supple frames for the fixed-pane windows; when drawn, they lightly veil the dramatic city skyline at night.

Previous page: Custom designed "doggie doors" recess into walls when not in use. *Right:* An onyx starburst-patterned floor and a full-wall mirror create welcoming grandeur, while a French Deco console and light fixtures add brightness and delicacy to the space.

The sleek lacquered afromosia wood paneling of the gallery showcases the clients' Judaica collection and then curves to frame the opening into the great room, which features a unique panorama of the New York skyline.

I detailed the apartment with French Deco accents to soften the modern architecture. In the living room, bas-relief metal panels frame the stunning city views, while the bronze-inlaid wood surfaces offer a nice counter to a collection of sumptuous French Deco pieces.

A large custom fixture of my design in bronze and onyx hovers above the Deco table. Motorized wall panels (shown closed) open up to the kitchen. Afromosia columns divide the dining room from the family room.

A pair of bifold doors in afromosia and brass recede into pockets at the entry to the den. The back wall, in sharkskin with brass inserts, provides a sensual backdrop for the extraordinary French Deco furniture.

The powder room is home to a custom-made rock crystal pedestal sink and a pair of elegant French Deco mirrors. A domed ceiling in gold leaf and black marble elevates the small space, while the onyx floor and walls add subdued glamour.

In the master bedroom, walls in pale parchment imbue it with a sense of serenity. The carpet, bed, night tables, and bench at the foot of the bed are all of my design.

At the north end of the master bedroom, a Chinese Coromandel screen provides a bold foil for French Deco furniture. Macassar ebony wood paneling was used to frame the window and entry openings.

Lalique inserts on the door of the master bath offer instant drama, further enhanced by the onyx and Belgian black marble floors. A sycamore vanity cabinet provides balance with its meticulous geometry and cool finish.

INTERNATIONAL DESIGN CENTER, ESTERO, FLORIDA, 2006

When I was named artistic director of the International Design Center in Estero, Florida, I recognized it as an opportunity to offer other interior designers what I judged to be missing in similar showroom buildings. My role here was a new one: I was neither architect nor interior designer. My mission was to give an overall look to the Center, bringing my own aesthetic to bear while allowing others who held those titles to execute its design.

Working within the architectural parameters of the building, I focused on the usage of the public areas, imagining overall proportions and the allotment of space. I was at liberty to give more attention to elements that are important to me, like the arrival sector and the main atrium. At the same time, I took an interest in aspects of the detailing by selecting various materials and finishes, and even dictating some of the hardware.

The facade of the building is neoclassically inspired, a beautiful envelope for a commercial purpose. Its symmetrical wings are fronted by a long colonnade, mirrored by allées of royal palms and a corridor of fountains. The plans begged for an entry that lived up to that experience. I created a magnificent pair of doors that would both invite curiosity about what lay beyond and symbolize the kind of custom, sometimes artisanal, work showcased inside. I selected hand-hammered copper plates as the skin for the doors and had them mounted irregularly in a sculptural fashion.

I worked on the reception room just inside the copper doors, intending it to be welcoming but also to build expectation. It has a gently vaulted ceiling sheltering a lineup of curvilinear chairs. I saw this as a contained space, with the feel of a tunnel that has light beyond. Just past the reception desk, the space immediately opens up onto the three-story atrium, creating surprise with the contrast in scale. At one end of this light-filled, covered courtyard, I detailed a rusticated tower of stone that houses the glass elevators and underlines its verticality.

While the Design Center is primarily an assemblage of showrooms through which to circulate and shop, I also made provision for contemplative areas. I called for multiple seating groups where professionals could pause and think awhile, meet their clients, or even spread out plans on the spot to work quietly. Based on my own experience, I knew they would welcome integrated "stops" to make sense of what they had seen, and meditate on their visions of how to use it.

Previous page: Logo of the International Design Center. *Right:* At the main entrance, patinated copper doors of my design open onto a welcoming reception room.

In the three-story atrium, a custom floor in three different marbles—white thassos, black absolute, and yellow aliednite—becomes a mirror for the profusion of light from the all-glass vaulted ceiling. The stone and glass elevator tower in the rear offers a vertical counterbalance to the ceiling.

Under a coved ceiling of anigre wood, comfortable custom lounges await visitors in the reception area. A floating desk in tiger wood echoes the curves of the chairs.

I detailed the front entrance door panels of patinated copper with bronze pulls and copper nail heads.

BEACH HOUSE, GOLDEN BEACH, FLORIDA, 2006

More than any other recent project of mine, this house is one I would dub eclectic. Some people are uncomfortable with that word, but I'm not. Eclecticism involves creativity, imagination. It's not about random busy-ness; it's about spinning visual intrigue from the unexpected.

On this project, a house by the Intracoastal Waterway on the Atlantic side of Florida, the owners asked for something traditional. I proposed a marriage of styles—soft, with historic roots, yet modern enough to mesh with their indoor-outdoor lifestyle. I collaborated with the architect on both the building and the landscape, and we produced a gracious, Mediterranean-style ensemble, but one with light-hearted touches: a waterside home in a warm climate doesn't want to be heavy or overly formal.

Ocean and sky were the touchstones for the color scheme: pale blues, teals, with darker tints here and there, and dabs of yellow. Blue runs like a river through the house, from the splash and countertop in the kitchen to the floral pattern of the living room sofa, the painted furniture of the dining room, and the bedroom textiles. The first pop comes in the airy, double-height front hall, where the aqua in the painting contrasts with the creamy palomino tones of the floor and stairs. The sweeping, curved staircase is crowned with a railing of curlicued metalwork, which is echoed in the iron bench and frieze of trees on the wall.

Other spaces continue to offer the eye unpredictable combinations. In the dining room, delicate antique Italian consoles socialize with an elaborate Dutch chandelier and silk-clad straight-back chairs. In the master bedroom, an amusing houndstooth table stands by a traditional upholstered bed with a large-scale check duvet. The walnut-paneled library mixes an overstuffed loveseat, two Deco leather chairs, and a contemporary metal-lattice cube table.

Outside, the home's Mediterranean heritage shines brightly. Sheltered by a gracious arcade, one can dine alfresco under lazy ceiling fans, gazing at an intricate Moorish-inspired tile wall or at the forest of tropical plants that serves as a luxuriant backdrop to the pool.

Previous page: Lush tropical plants and a red brick entryway help to inspire a Mediterranean demeanor. *Right:* A delicate metal balustrade delineates the sweeping staircase in the front hall. A painting by Donald Sultan and a crystal and metal Swedish chandelier by Erik Höglund (c. 1960) accentuate the height of the space.

In the dining room, a rare pair of eighteenth-century Italian gilt consoles plays well against an elaborate Dutch chandelier and French Louis XVI silk-backed chairs.

The blues of nature punctuate the living room, in a painting by María de la Paz Jaramillo and in upholstered sofas of my design. A Lalique fixture, pair of Deco lacquer columns, and textile artwork by Colombian artist Olga de Amaral add sensual accents. On the custom stone coffee table, a chocolate box sculpture by Peter Anton and a chess sculpture by Arman.

French country elements imbue the kitchen with warmth and color. Chairs from Holly Hunt enliven an antique French farm table, while a custom-tiled backsplash and a collection of antique pewter enrich the setting.

Under an elegant arcade, Moorish-style tile, low-hanging ceiling fans, and wicker furniture from Janus et Cie inspire an afternoon of alfresco leisure.

The tranquil waters of the Intracoastal serve as the color link to the master bedroom. A delicate Art Nouveau light fixture, a houndstooth table, and an assortment of patterns create layers of intriguing tension.

RUE JACOB PIED-À-TERRE, PARIS, 2005

My pied-à-terre in Paris is in an eighteenth-century building constructed before the Revolution, during the time of Louis XVI. It's on Rue Jacob, where the apartment buildings were put up not for aristocrats but for the poor. When I first laid eyes on the place it was a shambles: no kitchen and no bathroom to speak of, none of the walls parallel, countless ancient layers of paint that had to be removed. I was captivated nevertheless, because its charms were equally abundant—a pair of French doors opening onto a terrace overlooking a courtyard, 13-foot ceilings in the living room, beautiful hand-hewn old beams.

The pleasure here was in taking a small, archaic, higgledy-piggledy space and giving it coherence and character, using linear perspective as an organizing principle. One key move was to redo the floors, which had several different surfaces including a terribly busy *parquet de Versailles* in the living room. I chose long antique planks, in keeping with the age of the building, and placed them end to end throughout the apartment to give a feeling of continuity. From the entryway, the eye is drawn straight down the corridor, and the planks help lead it to the French doors, offering sunlight and a glimpse of greenery outside, as in a painting from the cinquecento.

In modernizing the space, I aimed for architecture that would feel smooth and clean while preserving the roughness of the antique elements. A new wall of scored wood panels behind the fireplace conceals storage space to house the TV and books. At the end of the living room opposite the terrace there's a sliding door, suspended from a track on the ceiling, that can close off any of three openings—to the bedroom, the kitchen, or the entry corridor. One wall in the kitchen has a blackboard-paint finish for doodling or jotting a shopping list in chalk. In the neoclassical-inflected bathroom, I designed a giant mortar for a sink and placed it on a columnal vanity in a soaring arched niche.

The color scheme runs from stark whites to taupes, including one with a bit of yellow in it. In the bedroom, however, more dramatic darks prevail. The wall is cut in two by a decorative molding in Macassar wood, inlaid with bone. Above that line, the surface is painted in a shade like café au lait; below it, the upholstered woods and bed treatment bring to mind the richest French *chocolat chaud*. As in the other rooms, sensuous refinement trumps the modest dimensions.

Previous page: In the living room, a Jean Arp sculpture (1958–60) rests on a cabinet of my design in lacquer and sharkskin.

Right: Antique wood flooring, a convex French antique mirror, and fixtures in plaster by Manuela Zervudachi lead the way down this narrow hallway to the living room.

An oversized sofa in white cotton serves as a neutral base for an eclectic assemblage of pieces: nineteenth-century Scandinavian armchairs, dining chairs from the Musée Rodin, a Louis XVI architect's desk, a slate-topped coffee table of my design, and glass stars by Finnish artist Oiva Toikka. On the terrace, a bronze sculpture by Émile-Antoine Bourdelle. Uniting the setting: a graphite drawing on canvas by Matsutani (1998).

Above: A 1950s ashtray by Stig Lindberg sits atop my slate-topped coffee table in the living room.
Right: An aluminum slice chair by Mathias Bengtsson and a bronze and linen sculpture by Manuela Zervudachi add texture to the fireplace and white painted wood panels.

Le beau est toujours bizarre
"Baudelaire"
et les Japonaises aussi

UNCONCERNED BUT NOT INDIFFERENT

The blackboard wall in the kitchen allows me to indulge my whims and offers a playful counter to wenge wood cabinetry, Belgian marble countertops, and a collection of antique Swedish and French copper objects.

Above: A bedroom niche features a tribal torso in biscuit porcelain.
Right: Sumptuous textures define my bedroom: a horsehair headboard, dark brown velvet wall covering, a chair rail in Macassar with bone inlays, rock crystal lamps. Hat molds that were transformed into mirrors hang above.

To subtly undercut the neoclassical elements in my bathroom, I converted a mask by Robert Courtright into a faucet and designed a limestone sink in the shape of a traditional mortar. The sink rests on a cabinet of my design; to the left, a French nineteenth-century cabinet with a marble top.

UPPER EAST SIDE RESIDENCE, NEW YORK CITY, 2005

What do you do when your children grow up and begin to move out? You streamline your life—and your living space. These clients live in a large Upper East Side apartment that I designed for them years ago. What they wanted then was highly traditional: sumptuous, ornate, baroque. But lives and tastes change, and after their older children left, they were ready for something new. They wanted a home more articulated and modern, more like the lofts that have so revolutionized home design in New York and elsewhere.

For me it's a thrill to approach a space I designed and reimagine it from the floor up. My key concept here was openness—the rooms flowing into one another, with longer sightlines. The ebonized floor in the ample living area extends into the library and the dining room, linking all three. I created "archways" by using a stand-alone fireplace to separate the dining room from the living room, while the wide entry into the library can be closed off with sliding doors. In the living space, the white upholstery and the lacquer table appear to float on the dark wood floor. The pieces here and elsewhere have a midcentury modern look, and many are from that period—perfect for the open-plan loft aesthetic.

The husband is an ambassador, the wife a philanthropist; both work and entertain at home. The sliding doors of the library allow the husband complete privacy when he needs it, or a wide-open feeling of connection. We carefully worked out the view from the living room into the library: a symmetry of consoles, mirrors, and vases on either side of the pocket doors, culminating in a pop of red from the Ward Bennett table on casters, his desk. The area rug grounds the table with a bold herringbone pattern.

For the bedroom, I reinterpreted a design I did in an old apartment of mine that the wife had seen and loved. Behind the bed, I placed a screen three-quarters the height of the room. On the other side of the screen there's an office, so she can work at night without disturbing her husband.

Previous page: The elevator foyer, elegantly wrapped in paper, is accessorized with a mirror and console from the 1950s and a pair of sconces purchased in Paris. *Right:* For the entrance hallway I painted the walls to resemble limestone and designed the wood floor, all to set off an exquisite 1930s Swedish table by Otto Wretling and a pair of Murano pendant lamps.

In the living room I used a neutral furniture base and a black pony-hair rug to highlight the extraordinary art and design: a coffee table by Marc Newson, a bronze sculpture by Fernando Botero, and a mixed-media composition by Venezuelan artist Jesús Soto. On the wall in the hallway, a collage by Sophia Vari.

The cerused oak doors of the library recede to show off a Ward Bennett table on casters. Flanking the doors is a pair of crest-shaped mirrors and leather-covered console tables. Behind, walls were painted to resemble parchment.

A 1920s dining table and 1940s Murano glass chandelier and glass sconces infuse the dining room with elegance, while the custom leather tufted chairs and the painting and library sculpture by Manolo Valdés add touches of warmth.

Two round tables in cherry and parchment that I designed punctuate the tonal neutrality of the master bedroom. A custom linen screen headboard with nail-head detail completes the composition.

PARK AVENUE APARTMENT, NEW YORK CITY, 2004

Candela and Carpenter: To the cognoscenti, the two names conjure up the essence of grandeur in classic New York apartment buildings. In the interwar decades, architects Rosario Candela and James Carpenter designed nearly 130 structures, often filled with 10- to 20-room apartments, graciously proportioned and brilliantly laid out.

My clients for this project, a couple in their early forties with children, bought a flat in an elegant Candela and Carpenter building on Park Avenue. He's a businessman and she's a mover and shaker in the philanthropy world. She wanted a home where they could entertain abundantly for her causes, so our goal was to infuse the traditional setting with glamour and to make every room a special experience.

The drama begins with the entry spaces. I made the elevator hall into a little gift package by tinting the walls and ceiling a metallic gray and turning up the glitter with a big mirror and slender brass console. I removed part of the wall at the far end of the foyer and placed two columns on either side of the new opening to frame the passage to the rest of the rooms.

The living room lies along the central axis of the space. Standing in its center, you enjoy views through grand mahogany doors into the library and dining room. Each of the three areas is done in a distinct style: the living room is rather old-world, with ornate touches; the dining room is glamorous, with its high-polish Deco table and chandelier like a host of icicles reflected in the mirror; the library is contemporary, with effects, like the generous use of leather, that call to mind an exclusive club.

A variety of background surfaces add panache. The living room was already paneled in English walnut, which my clients wanted to celebrate. To play against it, I had the ceiling painted in a grid pattern with silvers and golds. In the library I used a grid again, but this time on a wall of rich ruby leather. In the master bedroom parchment-clad closets fill one wall, and the window walls behind the bed are covered in two layers of fabric—one gauzy, to let light filter in by day, the other opaque, to create the feeling of sleeping in an opulent, private tent at night.

Previous page: In the entrance hallway, a mirror in a colonial-style carved frame, fabricated in Colombia, reflects a painting by Victor Matthews, a bronze sculpture by Arthur Dupagne (c. 1930), a glass and wood Japanese lantern converted into a ceiling fixture. *Right:* I created drama in this entrance hallway by widening the opening to the bedroom corridor and flanking it with new columns. Sculptural bronze side tables are by Philip Laverne, and the gilt bronze console by Raymond Subes.

The beautiful existing English walnut paneling in the living room was both an important feature and a challenge. To brighten the room I had the ceiling painted in silvers and golds. Painting by Wilfredo Lam.

In the library, rich red leather upholstered panels provide a dramatic backdrop for the seating arrangement. The parchment and brass coffee table, hexagonal table lamps, and silk and wool rug are all my design. The Deco desk and club chairs are French.

In the dining room, the original wall paneling, with a decorative new finish, provides an elegant frame for a French Deco dining table in Macassar ebony and a Venini glass chandelier designed by Carlo Scarpa (c. 1955). The existing parquet floors were stripped and stained to a much darker color that de-emphasizes the parquet pattern. The mahogany dining chairs are of my design.

In the master bedroom suite, wall-to-wall silk window treatments provide a serene backdrop for the bed and upholstered daybed by Tommi Parzinger (c. 1950). The wool and silk rug is one of my designs.

SOUTH BEACH FLAT, MIAMI BEACH, FLORIDA, 2003

It was 1994. Magazines and fashion designers had loads of models running down to South Beach to be photographed. The old Miami Beach was disappearing, but its Art Deco District was becoming a destination with architectural preservation in the air. I had, and have, lots of clients in the area and I was growing weary of booking into hotels that couldn't keep me if I needed to stay extra days when a job called for it.

I discovered a wonderful old seven-story apartment building in the Deco area called The Helen Mar, which was famous in the 1930s because Esther Williams had occupied the top floor. What's more, the building is located on the canal with a view of the ocean. I fell for it and bought two studio apartments, which when joined gave me a usable 1,500 square feet.

The apartment isn't large, but structural changes made it feel spacious. After knocking out the walls between the two studios, I was able to fashion an airy "bridge" between them by means of a permanent latticework screen. The door and pass-through openings in the lattice serve as a transition from the comfortable living room to an open kitchen and dining area, as well as to the ample bedroom beyond.

Focal points are important to visually organize a space of this size. The front door opens onto the strong silhouette of an oversized vase on a woodblock pedestal, next to a large white sphere. The shapes are backed up by a minimalist painting I did years ago, a pure expression in oils of volume and form. To the right, the living room beckons with a striking primitive painting that draws the eye to the far wall. To the left, the trellis pulls the gaze through with a translucency that indicates there is more to the apartment but creates a bit of mystery about what lies beyond: a tidy trick in a small space.

When I first decorated the rooms, they were very Miami, very colorful. But I soon tired of them and, several years ago, created instead a neutral zone, a calm place where I could withdraw after working with so many swatches and samples in the day-to-day. The living room is now done in tones of sand, tempered by large swaths of black and white. The bedroom is rich brown, with the aspect of a shady retreat at the end of a long day in the Florida sun. The decor is decidedly eclectic: African artwork and rustic materials establish a primitivism, but it is sharpened up with the definitive outlines of contemporary cabinetry and upholstery. With its cool backdrop of neutral hues and textural mix, the apartment now reflects a very different Miami, equally vibrant yet in a more subdued, sophisticated manner.

Previous page: A 1930s concrete garden urn rests atop an exotic wood pedestal in my entryway. The background painting is a work of mine done in Paris in the 1970s. *Right:* In the living room, an Old Mill stone, a rhinoceros in solid bronze, and a bronze torso create a compelling composition.

In the living room, a mélange of nationalities and periods: an eighteenth-century armoire from China, nineteenth-century cane chairs from Cambodia, nineteenth-century chairs from the Philippines, and a large oil painting by Hugo Bastidas (1999). The faux finished egg tables are of my own design.

To divide the living room from the kitchen, I built a trellis partition in ebonized wood. On a nineteenth-century Chinese console rests an early 1900s photo of a Turkish boy; behind is a nineteenth-century pharmacy cabinet from Sri Lanka.

In my bedroom, neutrals set off my collection of artwork (by Louise Bourgeois, Robert Courtright, Omar Rayo, William T. Hillman, and Karen Butler Connell) and a 1950s lamp in metal and wood. At left, an early Deco chair in rosewood with ivory inlays.

BEACH HOUSE, PUNTA CANA, DOMINICAN REPUBLIC, 2003

Two families, one house. A younger couple with children, and their parents. How do they coexist with the right balance of privacy and togetherness? In this case I was asked not just to design the interiors of the home but to do the architecture as well. My clients, the young couple, wanted a house inspired by traditional Spanish villas and colonial haciendas, a style that calls up a host of memories from my youth in Colombia.

I also knew the clients well—I had worked on homes for them in New York and Venezuela. They bought land in Punta Cana, in the Dominican Republic, for a vacation house. First they invited me down to size up the site. It's a long, narrow plot fronting on the ocean. I looked around, did some quick, naive sketches—and came up with what today is the house. My idea was to build a home shaped like a U and give each couple most of a wing: one for the young family, with kids' rooms and play rooms, and the other side for their parents, with an office and a sitting room. Then there are the common areas: kitchen, living room, dining room, video room, and the real heart of the home, the open-air living area between the courtyard and the pool.

This is a seaside house in the tropics, a take-off-your-shoes, no-need-for-formality house. The fundamentals here are Coralina stone floors, sun-filled spaces, the sound of water, and easy-care fabrics—all enhanced by heavy beams, dark colonial furniture, and stark white walls.

I always want arrival to feel like an adventure, so I placed the driveway to one side of the property and twisted it through lush plantings. You enter upon a series of corridors, inner and outer, and then encounter a huge double door opening onto a courtyard with a reflecting pool, small fountains as in the Alhambra, and a riot of tropical trees and shrubs. The courtyard draws the eye through to the other end of the house, where you can glimpse the ocean.

There's a constant interplay between inside and outside. For example, the ochre stucco I chose for the exterior wraps around and flows into the courtyard, creating the inner walls of the open-air living space, with its 25-foot ceilings. And if you fancy a break from the sun, or if a rain shower rolls in? Lower the three giant shades that descend from the exaggerated, Indonesian-influenced roof. The home is both gracious and flexible, comfortably embracing the needs of the three generations that occupy it.

Previous page: A carved sphere of Coralina stone and a hurricane lamp candleholder of my design separate the pool area from the ocean. The steps and interior of the pool are also of Coralina stone. *Right:* For the entrance to the house, I designed Spanish colonial style wood doors that open onto a lush inner courtyard. The hanging wrought iron lamps were made by local craftsmen.

A view of the inner courtyard. Local palm trees and vegetation flank the linear fountain, home to tropical fish. Alhambra-style water jets crisscross each other. The wood-clad wall on the second floor was done in a vernacular style called "clavot."

In the double-height great room, daybeds and chairs of my design were made locally. Arrangements of coconuts and flowers share the two large coffee tables with an antique African warrior woodcarving. Above the doors leading to the living room, my 10-foot-diameter mirror reflects the light.

In the dining room, darkly stained wood floors, doors, and ceiling beams provide an elegant contrast to the bright exterior, white stuccoed walls, and stone server of my design. Three square tables of my design (two are shown) can be arranged individually or combined for a more formal seating arrangement.

Flanking the double-height open-air great room are the air-conditioned living and dining rooms; the terraces of the two master bedrooms can be seen above. The massive wood shingle roof is supported by four 25-foot columns.

The south-wing master bedroom has a wraparound terrace overlooking the ocean. Soft, white fabrics and local perrilla-style stucco on the walls contrast with the dark andiroba wood floors and full-height window doors. A painting by Wilfredo Lam hangs above the bed.

In the guest bedroom, Anglo-Indian-style and rattan furniture create a light, tropical feel. Solid shutters on the windows control the light coming into the room.

COUNTRY HOUSE, ROXBURY, CONNECTICUT, 2003

The old, the new. Often in a design project one must search for inventive ways to balance the two. At this site, my solution was to strip away layers of the past until only the best remained, and then build a new structure to happily coexist with it.

I had worked with this family for years when they bought a property in rural Connecticut. The 1805 farmhouse had been expanded numerous times, until the original became lost in the additions. I suggested that instead of trying to work with it, we demolish everything but the original saltbox, convert it to a guesthouse, and create a new "barn" for their main residence.

The lines of the historic house, stripped of its add-ons, are clean and balanced. We elongated the front windows into a row of French doors, and a terrace now fronts the facade. The white clapboard structure stands by the long driveway like a welcoming host, inviting the visitor to either pause and settle in or continue 'round to the main house behind. Inside, the saltbox's soul is that of a nineteenth-century farmhouse—broad plank floors, old fireplaces, furniture spare and understated—but contemporized with a stylish wink.

For the barn-look-alike home, we found a highly skilled specialist who collects and uses recycled barn wood, adapting vernacular outbuilding models to new construction. A plan emerged, an elastic rendering of a typical farm building, to accommodate an active family with a longing for space. On the exterior, I employed a muted brown-red stain made from natural pigment, a formula used in Sweden, rather than the brighter American shade. Instead of calling out the windows with contrasting white trim, I had most of them painted out in the overall color, helping the large dwelling's volume to recede so as not to upstage the historic guesthouse.

The interior of the barn hews to the rustic ethos, with a huge fieldstone fireplace and high chimney as its centerpiece. The clients had seen my expansive room at the Villa Maria Show House (page 170), and I proposed modifying some of those ideas for the furnishings. The custom coffee table, sofas, and club chairs, arranged in multiple groupings, are oversized in keeping with the room's proportions, as is the refectory table in the dining room. Structural beams bisect the walls, and art is hung both above and below, helping to press the soaring ceiling height down to a cozier scale. Throughout, craft- and folk-inspired objects mesh comfortably with modern works, while rugged exposed beams and barn board provide a backdrop for soft custom seating—the old holding hands with the new.

Previous page: A composition of nineteenth-century objects in the living room of the guesthouse, dated 1805. *Right:* In the library, reclaimed white oak plank flooring provides a solid foundation for a custom sofa in crewel fabric, a vintage red leather wingchair with nail-head trim, and an antique bench, used as a coffee table.

For the exterior of the main "barn" house, I used a muted brown-red stain made from earth pigment and painted out the windows, to avoid upstaging the historic guesthouse. A sculpture by Francisco Narváez rests behind the horses.

In the living room, a 10-foot-long sofa of my design and equally wide coffee table counterbalance the soaring ceiling. Folk art and rugged exposed beams also help to humanize the substantial space.

An oak refectory table, iron fixtures, and fieldstone fireplace
create a genial setting for family meals; a seventeenth-century
Guatemalan archangel sculpture watches over the festivities.

Recycled wood and folk-inspired objects infuse the expansive kitchen with unaffected warmth, while the industrial light fixtures add a modern touch.

A granite fireplace creates an indulgent focal point in the master bedroom offset by an antique Oriental rug. The plump upholstered furniture, wall sconces, and metal canopy bed are of my design.

White linens and a white bathtub elegantly refresh the master bathroom's recycled wood. Industrial lighting adds a subtle counterpoint.

MADISON AVENUE APARTMENT, NEW YORK CITY, 2003

Nestled above the surrounding buildings, my New York apartment is long on light but, typical for Manhattan, a bit short on space. It is filled with works of art and certain furniture silhouettes I am flirting with for wider production. Indeed, I like to use my own home as an incubator of ideas. This one challenged me to glamorize a traditional layout via chiaroscuro and scale, and to exercise my ingenuity in devising multiuse solutions.

I decided on a dramatic black and white scheme—to paint out certain areas so they would recede, allowing others to pop. The use of black is a definite design stroke with an indefinite effect: You feel an infinite line; edges become undistinguishable. I chose this color for the walls of the entry, which in turn leads your eye directly into the brighter living room: the black bends around onto the wall behind the couch. A 10-foot-long white sofa against an all-black backdrop is commanding in a room that is otherwise a study in whites.

In the living area the space opens up, so I created excitement by calling attention to the change in scale. In addition to the oversized sofa, I specified floor-to-ceiling folding screens and a large graphic painting, which offers the only punch of color in the otherwise neutral room. I had the pair of screens fabricated, faced with pressed tin, and painted black, like the one wall. They are a key component, used to bookend the couch and catch the light, adding alluring texture and a bit of architecture (where there is none). Within this same room—used for both living and dining—I had a series of tall bookcases built in to define a dining corner.

I employed the crescent-shaped lounge chairs around the coffee table to soften the angularity of the other furniture. This is a shape I use over and over—it's my own design—because the dark wood frames of these chairs against tufted white upholstery sharpens their outline and literally throws a curve in any room. Circles represent a sense of continuity to me, the kind of flow I like to underscore in my interiors.

Fortunately, the scale of this one-bedroom flat did nothing to inhibit my choice of art objects. I find that substantial pieces add even more character when the space is modest. My strategy is to go against the grain: the apartment becomes grander with grand pieces. Further, the black and white scheme, leavened with the warm-white parchment of some of the cabinet work, serves as the perfect foil for not just art but also for my ever-changing collection of books.

Previous page: A cast iron torso by Spanish artist Xavier Mascaró resides in my living room. *Right:* In a corner, a black metal console of my design shows off a bronze by Manolo Valdés and a plaster shell by an anonymous artist. A graphite drawing by David Roth adds dimension to the tableau; a pressed-tin screen and bronze lamp by Just Andersen provide vertical counterweights. Bronze egg by Lucio Fontana; zebra plate by Jean Lambert-Rucki.

The constraints of the low ceilings and fairly small dimensions of my living area are minimized by a dramatic black and white color scheme. The sleigh chairs, metal coffee table, and carpet are all of my design. The graphic painting is by Charles McMurray, lithograph by Lucio Fontana, loop sculpture in background by Eva Hild, and ceramic vase by Pol Chambost.

I am an avid collector of art and art objects. Here, a painting by Manolo Valdés and a drawing by Rufino Tamayo provide the backdrop for my collection of decanters and carafes, a nineteenth-century silver pitcher from Colombia, and a silver sculpture by Salvador Dalí.

Built-in bookcases in white lacquered wood and parchment hold my collection of books and define the dining corner. The wood table and slipcover chairs are of my design. A bronze sculpture by Jean Gabriel Chauvin and stemware by Lalique add touches of subdued glamour.

In a study of neutrals, a splash of red offers the element of surprise. The armoire and chests are of my design. A circle sculpture by Bruno Romeda and a leg sculpture by Xavier Mascaró balance on an antique Chinese table. The wall behind the bed is covered with a cotton canvas panel, accented with nail heads.

VILLA MARIA SHOW HOUSE, WATER MILL, LONG ISLAND, 2002

One spring, I was offered a place in a designer show house that was to be held in Villa Maria, a glorious nineteenth century estate in Water Mill, formerly used as a convent. My eye was immediately drawn to the biggest room in the house, 35 feet wide by 60 feet long, with a riveting view of Mecox Bay. I put forth the obvious question: How do you create a scheme for a room of such magnitude? Answer: Custom-design everything in it, and step up the scale.

I allowed myself to be guided by the inherent symmetry and great character of the room. Visually, I divided the space in two halves, which I treated similarly yet not identically. Each was furnished utilizing the repetition of certain elements, but I played with variations in shape and scale. Joining the halves is a huge refectory table that serves as a pivotal piece. When you want to have extravagant dinners, this center table becomes a buffet. When meals are more intimate, it can be attractively laid with individual place settings. For everyday use, it becomes a handsome display surface piled with books and curios. The table controls the movement of the room, the circulation.

I anchored each end of the space with a sofa and substantial coffee table. These tables are made from weighty lengths of wood that resemble railroad ties belted with iron. I floated a daybed between each coffee table and the central refectory table. The low daybeds extend the seating without blocking the main axis; they help the room read as a whole. In one corner I positioned two big, overstuffed chairs that could be delicious for an afternoon nap, although they're there for playing backgammon or chess.

The room has great bones with proportions that are called out by the exposed wood. I made the moldings, ceiling beams, and posts at the windows even more prominent by having them stained dark and finished to a high polish. There's a marvelous fireplace of carved plaster that rises to the full height of the 12-foot ceiling, which itself is textured with beautiful, carved plasterwork.

This is a room in which I wanted to create a sense of possibility: Come into the space and move around. Use it for entertaining. Form different conversation groups and have different pastimes. Because of the attention I've given to scale and repetition, it has a rhythmic feel. Like a musical composition, it is all-of-a-piece yet made up of varying segments. The room can be seen as strong and masculine, with bold lines and vigorous volumes. But its crisp whites also make it ladylike and so very right for the Hamptons.

Previous page: A painting by Manolo Valdés on an antique easel is flanked by sconces of my design. *Right:* Strong shapes and diverse textures that harmonize create visual intrigue. Artwork by Antonio Tapies on walls specially treated with Venetian plaster. The shell plaster sculpture is by an anonymous artist. Deer sculpture in background by Walter Rotan.

A large-scale sofa and tufted daybed, both of my design, pop when bordering an oversized darkly stained wood coffee table. Sheer shades in parchment-colored linen are also of my design. Circle sculpture by Bruno Romeda.

A central refectory table anchors the room and provides the
perfect base for an intriguing still life. A sculpture in marble
by Igor Mitoraj is balanced by a nineteenth-century wood finial
from New Orleans.

A pair of wicker chairs with loose cotton cushions relax by the fireplace, which is stacked with white birch. A white cowhide rug offers additional textural intrigue.

Oversized linen arm chairs invite conversation or relaxation,
while a metal table, iron lamp, and dark-stained bookcase with a
light blue interior, all of my design, allow for multiple distractions.

POOL HOUSE, GARRISON, NEW YORK, 2002

For two years after I bought this wooded property—with the thought that someday it would be my home—I simply looked at the trees. I felt a deep respect for how the environment had evolved and decided to consider carefully before making my imprint. First, I set to work on the brook that runs through the land, which had been destroyed by time and neglect. Next, I dammed the lake and stocked it with bass and trout, and for many years, even after the house was built, I happily swam there among the snapping turtles.

Eventually, it became apparent that my guests didn't uniformly share my enthusiasm. So I went to work on a pool. What started out as an idea for a pool house off to one side gradually took shape in my mind as a unique open-air space. The notion allowed me to provide for more than the expected amenities and freed me from the visual constraints of the usual pool house. My solution is a rustic stone construction that moors the swimming area, creates a wind break, and camouflages a changing room—all while paying homage to the natural setting.

The roofless, masonry structure stands in the footprint of the more conventional outbuilding I first imagined. At first glance it resembles a ruin. Its rough-cut stones are carefully piled without mortar, following the model of the old, low walls used historically by farmers in this part of the country to mark property lines. But these walls precisely frame the view from inside the enclosure toward the pool, and also from the pool back toward an outdoor hearth. The firebox is massive, about 7 feet high; by contrast, a fountain sunk in the center of the stone floor is slight. There are large chaises where one can recline and reflect in the presence of the primal: fire, water, and air.

This swimming and lounging area, situated halfway up the hill between the lake and the house, required extensive grading to settle it in the landscape. For the floor of the pool, I adapted a pattern that caught my eye in one of Sweden's royal palaces. Its precision echoes the geometric profile of the stone enclosure. Despite appearances, guests do have a place to shower and dress in a room concealed from poolside, in an extension behind the fireplace.

Previous page: The bucolic spillway from the three-acre lake. *Right:* Local granite provides the foundation for the patio by the pool, while a substantial firebox and sunken fountain complete the essential elements. Wire basket chairs by Tes Pasola.

The floor of my 60-foot pool was inspired by a pattern I had seen in a palace in Stockholm. Hurricane lanterns of my design help to punctuate the pattern's exquisite geometry.

The open-air structure merges with the natural setting. Metal daybeds of my design are padded with cotton canvas. Salt-glazed vessels on granite pedestals stand guard.

The cabana, hidden behind the fireplace. Dark-stained wood and bamboo wall covering create an exotic simplicity. A rectangular century-old American mirror counterbalances the porthole window.

UPSTATE NEW YORK RESIDENCE, POUND RIDGE, NEW YORK, 2001

Sometimes on a project, the chemistry is just right. When a couple called me out of the blue one Saturday at my country house, I was taken aback but curious. Who were they? How did they find me on a weekend afternoon? I decided to go see their house, not far from mine, in just as spontaneous a way as the offer had been extended. Our conversation was lighthearted and easy even before we got to discussing the work. We liked each other right away.

The house was another story. I found myself in a 1960s glorified ranch-style structure. The materials were rough-hewn granite and wood—the house nestled beautifully in the mature landscape—but the interior spaces were uncomfortably small and without stature. The clients, who had lived there for years, proposed I work with an architect they had engaged to enlarge the house. My job was to consult with him on the exterior and to play my accustomed role in opening up as well as appointing the interiors.

The house badly needed a point of view, a sense of arrival, a feeling of spaciousness. In the new plan, nature—omnipresent because of our strategic placement of large windows—and artwork define the entry. A series of corridors lead inward, allowing important art to capture your eye. Beyond, the house now opens to an expansive living room and dining room, separated only by a rustic yet modern stone hearth that allows free circulation between the two rooms. The freestanding fireplace brings the natural material inside, promoting continuity with the many window views of the exterior, and complements the wood ceiling.

The addition to the house gave me the space to get especially creative with the dining room and indulgent with the master bedroom. I designed a sleek kitchen-bar that runs the full length of the dining space, of fine wood so it reads like an elongated buffet. It becomes either a beautiful serving area for parties or a simplified preparation area for smaller meals. The master bedroom is luxurious in an understated way—a commodious living space that happens to encompass a sleeping area. One corner is dominated by important art, while practical functions are served by elegant seating elements and fastidiously crafted parchment and rosewood cabinetry.

Previous page: In the hallway gallery, Emile Bernard's *Portrait de Femme a la Chaise* (1930) watches over a rare settee by Ruhlmann.
Right: Artwork and antiques guide the visitor through the entry gallery, which connects the two wings of the house: palm wood and patinated bronze sideboard by Eugene Printz (c. 1935); Lalique "Tourbillons" vase (c. 1925); Boris Lovet-Lorski's *Venus* (1931); Art Deco rug by Ivan da Silva Bruhns.

In the living room, clean-lined furniture and window treatments allow the greenery and the antiques to take center stage: a rosewood and palissander cabinet and game table, both by Ruhlmann; Paul Dupré-Lafon's suite of four bridge chairs in ebonized wood; Otto Wretling's mechanical coffee table (1930). On top of cabinet, Rembrandt Bugatti's *Petit Leopard Marchant* sculpture.

Parchment and wenge built-in closets and credenzas elegantly set off a Ruhlmann lounge armchair in Macassar ebony with beige silk tapestry, a Deco rug by Ivan da Silva Bruhns, and René Buthaud's *Toilette de Venus* (c. 1930).

A Macassar ebony island elegantly unites the stainless steel kitchen and the dining area. Ruhlmann's dining chairs in Macassar ebony frame a Subes and Porteneuve ebony-and-gilt iron table. On the pedestal against the wall, Fernando Botero's *Seated Woman* (1987); on the table, Henri Laurens's *Femme au Bras Leveé* (1930).

PENTHOUSE DUPLEX, PARIS, 2001

I lived in Paris when I was young, I keep a pied-à-terre there now, and of course I do business there all the time. So it's especially rewarding whenever I'm asked to do a project in that city.

This one offered extra delights. The client is an American who wanted a base for his business visits to Paris. He bought a large penthouse duplex in a famous series of buildings constructed in 1925 by renowned architect Jean Walter. The structure is an Art Deco landmark. The client desired a space that would feel very French, very Parisian. So the basic approach was clear: focus on the Deco essence and create a home for a collection of important furniture from that period.

Upon entering the long, gallery-like foyer, one immediately encounters the mood and materials woven through the rest of the apartment. The space is austere, yet it has the warmth of wood. I designed an unusually deep molding, establishing a rhythm that brings continuity to all the main rooms, and together with applied "columns" offers a canvas for inlaid Deco motifs.

The window wall of the living room has a semi-hexagonal shape, which induces a sense of being embraced. I use the interplay of parchment panels, wood, and custom textiles to provide a backdrop for the art and stunning furnishings. A gold-leaf screen complements the seating, and two exquisite torchieres cast their glow on the ceiling. Around the fireplace, another grouping of armchairs is backed by woodwork inlaid with a diamond pattern that sets off a collection of African masks.

The angled walls in the dining room, in lighter tones of wood, echo those of the living area, giving the space a prismatic effect. Here the centerpiece is a one-of-a-kind Lalique table made for the Paris Exposition of 1925. It's flanked by striking works of art: a pair of sharply graphic black-and-white paintings and on the opposite wall, an Art Deco bas-relief.

I preserved the curvaceous staircase that leads up to the master suite and used it to help define a transitional space with a softly lit nook for reading and quiet moments. The bedroom is a medley of soft taupes and beiges, ceding pride of place to a romantic view of Paris rooftops.

Previous page: A 1930s French bas-relief hangs beyond the dining room table, while a bronze head of a bull by Josette Hebert-Coëffin (1940) rests atop. Behind, a Jacques Adnet console supports a Jean Besnard vase (1930). *Right:* In the foyer, a pair of lanterns by Jacques Quinet (1966) illuminate a Raymond Subes console (1950), a Jean Dunand plate (1915), and a Jean Besnard vase (1927). The round artwork on the wall is by Robert Courtright.

In the living room, parchment panels create an elegantly warm backdrop for the Deco art and furnishings: chairs in brown leather by Ruhlmann (1923) and in beige fabric by Jean Royère (1950); torchieres by Marc du Plantier (1936); a screen by Katsu Hamanaka; clay head by Jean Besnard (1932); and a vase by Maurice Gensoli.

Deco-inspired bookcases and a collection of African masks flank the living room fireplace. Chairs by Jean Royère (1950), a custom coffee table of my design, and a rug by Ivan da Silva Bruhns create a chic tableau. Floor lamp by Paul Dupré-Lafon. Painting by Serge Poliakoff.

In the library, substantial mahogany bookshelves set off the delicate lines of a Jean-Michel Frank sofa and chairs. A painting by François Cante-Pacos (1950) and a desk by Jacques Adnet (1950) add further visual intrigue.

An aesthetically quiet corner for reading or contemplation: coffee table by Jacques Adnet and Jacques Lenoble (1940), pair of chairs by André Sornay (1930), and a sofa from Holly Hunt. Painting by Jean Degottex (1967).

A pair of bold, oversized paintings by Victor Vasarely and Deco wall paneling of anigre wood offset the simplicity of a one-of-a-kind Lalique dining table made for the Paris Exposition of 1925. An alabaster chandelier from France (1930) and an Orrefors mirror offer subtle accents.

In the master bedroom, soft taupes and beiges provide an elegant backdrop for a desk by Paul Dupré-Lafon (1940), small lamp by Jean-Michel Frank, and small gouache painting by Christian Bérard (1950).

L'ÉTOILE OFFICE, PARIS, 2000

In the heart of Paris, a stone's throw from the Arc de Triomphe, a multinational corporation occupies space in an early-nineteenth-century building. The offices themselves had already been designed when the CEO of the company asked me to give the executive suite a different mood. The idea was to create a space that doesn't read as an office, but as something warmer, more like a home. My approach was to honor the traditional architectural fittings while playing them against modern furniture and art.

The suite consists of three rooms of diminishing size—a large meeting room, the CEO's personal office, and his secretary's space. In the meeting room, a series of tall French doors open onto a spectacular view of the Arc and let natural light flood in. They give the space a rhythm and sense of airiness that's picked up in the striking ceiling, carved and gilded, with an oval skyscape painted in the nineteenth century. The weighty Deco-inspired couch and chairs in the seating area offer grounding in counter-play to the ceiling motif, while the conference area is defined by a sleek table surrounded by a retinue of swivel chairs. An expansive Oriental carpet pulls the two sections together.

The French doors march on through the CEO's office, a study in warm neutrals: a Frank Lloyd Wright desk, Adnet chairs, a herringbone-pattern floor, and one wall upholstered in a set of squares that mirror the Robert Courtright metal painting on the opposite wall. The door leading into the secretary's space, constructed from pieced wood planks, emphasizes other verticals in the room—and mimics the tall niche nearby, with a bust that adds a classical touch to the otherwise modernist feel.

Previous page: A work on metal by Robert Courtright hangs above a pair of leather chairs by Adnet. *Right:* View from the secretary's office into the CEO's office. Venetian plaster walls highlight a bronze torso, a vase by Jean Dunand on a cherry wood pedestal, and a pair of leather chairs by Adnet.

Tall French doors and a view of the Arc de Triomphe provide the backdrop for the conference and sitting room, while mask sculptures by Robert Courtright watch over the proceedings. Leather and fabric chairs by Paul Dupré-Lafon; table by Eugene Printz; vase by Marguerite de Bayser-Gratry (1925).

The clean lines of a Knoll conference table and a Bruno Romeda
coffee table counterbalance both the restored original ceiling and
an antique Oriental rug. Metal and enamel vases by Jean Després.

The restored original mantel and mirror in the conference room
reflect an abstract painting by Georges Noël (1983).

UPPER EAST SIDE TOWNHOUSE, NEW YORK CITY, 2000

Occasionally it falls to someone in my line of work to serve as curator as well as designer. My clients on this project are prominent art collectors who bought a townhouse in New York, one of the largest in the city, built near the turn of the twentieth century. They hired an architect to gut it and reconfigure the layout. It includes a sizable kitchen and wine cave with adjacent dining space, a formal dining room, a large library, rooms for their three children, even a gym. Of critical importance to my task in imagining the rooms was the placement of the artwork, giving it a role in the house as central as it plays in these clients' lives.

The wife is from South America, and they're passionate about styles and periods of art ranging from pre-Columbian to African to classic modernism from both sides of the Atlantic. I used the lofty entrance hall to set the tone for the rest of the house, one of simplicity and muted color, with forceful artworks balanced by negative space and often used architecturally. The African sculpture placed on a pedestal there mirrors the strong verticals of the doorway to the dining room and the full-length portrait. The living room is also a clean white envelope designed to accommodate good conversation among friends, watched over by the ensemble of pre-Columbian figures on projecting metal stands.

In the library, a double-height room with a balcony, the essential issue was scale, so important in all my work. A powerful life-size African figure at one end humanizes the space, and instead of one chandelier, I used two, hanging them relatively low to create more intimate dimensions. Since the balcony acts as a bridge to one of the children's rooms, I devoted the upper section of the library to kids' books and the lower section to adults'. On the windows, here and elsewhere, wood-slat plantation blinds fold into the walls to afford views of the courtyard, or close to allow privacy and sun protection for the paintings.

Art is a key element even in the children's rooms, but naturally art of a different sort. A painter was commissioned to do murals of circus and Western scenes. I matched them with brightly colored, geometrically patterned furnishings and toys transformed into whimsical bedside lamps.

Previous page: Detail from the children's room. *Right:* In the entrance hall, overscaled limestone steps guide the eye to the dining room and beyond, encountering an array of sensual art along the way, including a carved African sculpture at left and a portrait by Diego Rivera in the background.

In the living room, the clients' collection of pre-Columbian artifacts offsets the linearity of the fireplace, sofas by Jean-Michel Frank, and coffee table by Paul Dupré-Lafon.

A painting by Roberto Matta adds verve to a quietly elegant conversational setting: chairs by Pierre Chareau; coffee table by Diego Giacometti; low cabinet by Paul Dupré-Lafon; vase on piano by Venini.

Double-height built-in bookcases accentuate the library's scale while low-hanging bronze chandeliers by Jean Royère work to humanize it. A carved African sculpture adds sensuality and soul. Coffee table by Carlo Mollino.

A dining table by Raymond Subes and chairs by Ruhlmann elegantly define the dining space. A Marisol Escobar sculpture watches over the festivities.

The wine cellar has ample space for a refectory table for dining and offers a dramatic view of the kitchen. Chairs by Gio Ponti.

A riot of color and fun marks the children's room, with a circus mural by Vesna Bricelj and painted furniture of my design.

OCEANFRONT APARTMENT, BAL HARBOUR, FLORIDA, 2000

An open living plan can be spectacular but making its design seem effortless often calls for unique maneuvers. Clients in Florida wanted their condominium apartment, high up in a new tower at the ocean's edge, to be converted to a luxury "loft" and to incorporate the brilliant view. With wraparound windows and a southeast exposure, the apartment had the potential to yield a gloriously light-filled space. My solution was to open up 2,000 square feet so that a seating arrangement, dining area, media room, and games table set-up would orbit around a pair of fixed columns.

I began by turning structural givens into assets. A hefty supporting column, exposed when I demolished the walls, became a pivot point. It now sports a faux marble finish, lending it dignity and blending it into the light hue of the walls and the pickled woodwork. Similarly, floor-to-ceiling pipes became the backbone of an entertainment platform. I housed them in an imposing, cone-shaped construction with a deep bronze finish, and built around it an elongated oval serving island for drinks and hors d'oeuvres.

For the enclosed foyer, I used highly detailed marble floors and oversized parchment doors to both heighten the drama upfront and set the visitor up for the continuous play of geometry and line beyond. Pewter gray grooved moldings begin here and subtly wrap their way through the open living area. I created a wide grid on the stone floor that leads from the entry, and positioned furniture and art to simulate a corridor within the open space.

Most of the furnishings are custom. Some shapes were inspired by the elliptical cone, and all of them reflect the interplay of circles and squares that fascinates me. The main seating area is anchored by a strong, rectangular metal and soapstone coffee table, which reiterates the shape of a large painting nearby. The circular dining table floats under a spherical chandelier near the window wall. To orient the furniture arrangements in the library/media area and master bedroom, I imposed a pattern of squares on cabinetry dividers and rectangles on a fabric-covered wall. I used plump upholstery, sheer drapes, and layered bedding to offset the geometric lines. The predominantly parchment-toned scheme, low seating horizons, and semitransparent table bases facilitate the flooding of light through the spacious, open plan.

Previous page: In the living room, a nineteenth-century Italian specimen table, inlaid with exotic stones, creates its own focal point. Game chairs of my design. *Right:* For the foyer, I designed highly geometric marble floors and parchment doors to create immediate drama. Silver leaf console and mirror by J. Robert Scott.

In the main seating area I balanced a bold painting by Maurice Ducret with a highly architectural iron and soapstone coffee table of my design. The pair of repoussé gilt metal lamps are also of my design.

A circular Karl Springer dining table and spherical Lalique chandelier are offset by chairs upholstered in an African-inspired fabric by Clarence House. Mixed media by Rufino Tamayo.

The light-filled "loft" space. I designed a spherical cone to hide a structural column and used it as the centerpiece for a center bar, in stainless with a deep bronze finish. Karl Springer swivel chairs in leather and mohair complete the tableau.

In the bedroom, a nineteenth-century Italian landscape adds gravitas to a contemporary setting: an ebonized wood coffee table; a pair of "Pisces" upholstered armchairs of my design; a marble sculpture by the owner.

I softened the geometric motif in the bedroom with a rectangular-patterned fabric-covered wall, framed in bamboo. The pair of lacquer and bronze night tables and Macassar bench are of my design.

For the powder room I turned a seventeenth-century French
stone fountain into a pedestal sink. Here, the use of geometric
forms on the door provides an unexpected counterpoint.

HARBOR VIEW APARTMENT, MIAMI BEACH, FLORIDA, 1999

How to make a modest-sized Miami apartment work as a top-flight gallery? First, invent imaginative ways to maximize display space. Second, place artworks everywhere—even on the balcony. My client for this project is an art dealer. He wanted a home in southern Florida—which was fast becoming an international hub for connoisseurs—where he could bring clients and informally exhibit. In other words, he didn't want it to look like a conventional flat. Part of my strategy was to lavish more attention on the walls than one might usually do in a smallish space.

In the living room, which doubles as the main showplace, one wall is covered in rattan, with molding employed to create symmetry. A series of panels can move to close off the other rooms or open them up, depending on the need. I designed a special system for the art so the paintings can be changed without marring the surface: slim rods hanging from channels at the top of the walls allow the works to be suspended and highlighted. This project demonstrates one of my favorite interior design paradoxes well: oversized art often makes a diminutive space seem grander.

The main seating area revolves around a large-scale ottoman, covered in raffia, which stands in for a coffee table. The chairs and sofa, all in neutrals, are non-matching, a composition that's strong enough to stand up to the art but doesn't compete. The rug is sisal and the walls tan, giving the room a warmer feel than the typical gallery white.

I splashed bright tints in the bedrooms. For the master, whose windows look out over the Intracoastal Waterway and lower Miami, I chose sea blue and floated the bed in the center. Primary-hued furniture in the guest bedroom adds pizzazz and picks up shades from the colorful canvases.

Previous page: Detail of a painting by Tony Scherman. *Right:* In the living room, a grasscloth wall covering adds texture to an ebony wall unit of my design. The chairs are contemporary in a light cotton fabric by Holland & Sherry.

Bold colors and interesting shapes create provocative tension in the guest bedroom: red leather chairs by Verner Panton; paintings by Maria Mercedes Hoyos and Stephen Conroy.

In the main seating area, a sofa in gray mohair by B&B, black 1950s leather chairs, and a raffia-covered ottoman speak to the art but don't compete with it. Artwork by Manolo Valdés (left) and Tony Scherman.

Geometric custom linens by Casa Del Bianco enhance
the sensuality of a charcoal painting by Fernando Botero.

LUXURY TOWER, PHILADELPHIA, PENNSYLVANIA, 1998

The setting: a grand apartment house in downtown Philadelphia. My clients bought three flats, aiming to combine them into one, and they called me because they had seen a project I had done for a family in the building. The interesting problem here was how to sensitively transform an elongated rectangular space with fairly low ceilings into living areas that felt at once roomy and logical.

The layout I designed features two entrances so that guests can enjoy the liberty of coming and going on their own. The guest suite occupies one end of the long rectangle, the master suite the other. The primary entrance leads into a majestic corridor running the length of the central living space, with floors in mariposa marble and structural columns clad in planes of green-gray onyx framed in ebony. I used ebony again in fashioning the hall's most striking element, the octagonal cutouts in the ceiling that mimic skylights but whose illumination flows from glowing lights installed behind a grid pattern of alternating horizontal and vertical slats. The outlines of the octagons are repeated on the floor, creating rhythmic visual stops.

A linear grid motif organizes the main living space as well—in the soffit lighting system, which relates to that of the recessed octagons; in the gently arched cove ceiling of lacquered wood coffers; in a built-in screen dividing the main "living room" from the dining room; and in the forged-iron standing lamps. The seating area is congenial, with custom benches and armchairs supplementing a sofa and a low daybed that allows for sightlines out the windows. In the dining room I employed two square tables instead of one large one, for seatings of eight or sixteen; for less formal meals en famille there's a light-bathed dining setting adjacent to the kitchen.

One curious element of this building's architecture is the series of window balconies that jut out like triangles from one long side of the apartment. What to do with them? During parties, they're perfect places for guests to mingle and admire the view. But for everyday living, I chose to close them off with translucent curtains to give the rooms cleaner lines—except in the master bedroom, where I left the triangular bay open and placed a plush chaise under a simple hanging globe to craft a seductive reading corner.

Previous page: In the guest foyer, a ceramic vase with a dark glaze finish rests on a Macassar console table of my design. *Right:* Walls of gray-green onyx with ebony trim set the mood of the primary entrance to the master's suite. The floor lamps in hammered iron are of my design. The screen in the back is attributed to Eileen Gray.

In the majestic entrance corridor, glowing lights from the octagonal cutouts in the ceiling are rhythmically repeated on the mariposa marble floors.

A built-in screen divides the main living space from the dining area, punctuated by an oversized rosewood pedestal supporting an alabaster urn. The coved ceiling offers an illusion of height for the elegant yet comfortable seating area. The inlaid panel on top of the coffee table is from the ship *Ile de France*.

The dining area fuses a variety of styles and periods: a Biedermeier armoire, a mid-twentieth-century Italian chandelier, Chinese-inspired chairs, and a table of my design. The soffit lighting along the perimeter recalls the Art Deco octagons of the entrance corridor.

I created a cozy reading and lounging corner in the triangular
bay off the master bedroom, with a quilted chaise, a late-
nineteenth-century hanging globe fixture, and lush curtains.

Subdued glamour continues in the master bedroom, with mohair wall panels, Murano glass lamps, and a Deco-inspired bed and night tables, of my design.

For the powder room, I turned a sixteenth-century French fountain into a pedestal sink and covered the walls in sherry with ebony trim and inserts of lapis lazuli.

FIFTH AVENUE RESIDENCE, NEW YORK CITY, 1998

The Sherry-Netherland, an Art Deco masterpiece built in 1927, has long been one of New York's most prestigious addresses—part hotel, part residence. My clients on this project had bought two flats; we combined them into one and essentially gutted and reconfigured the space. The apartment now occupies 3,500-plus square feet and is one of the most traditional I've ever done. The owners, clients of long standing, pictured old-world opulence that would showcase fine period antiques and a museum-quality art collection.

The first question for me is always: How does one approach the space? In the entryway, an imposing Giacometti head immediately makes a strong statement. The ceiling is coved and coffered, which lends a sense of movement and pattern. But the serenity of the room lets the statue and the demi-lune console, sporting a little Henry Moore, play the starring roles.

In the living room I deployed subtle architectural elements: deep triple moldings and decorative wood trim form panels on the walls that set off the paintings. The swagged drapes mimic the lines of the molding. A color palette of golds and ivories creates an understated glow, and the glints of gilt are reiterated elsewhere in the apartment. The tints, textiles, and pools of light cast by the lamps make the room feel soft and inviting.

The dining room posed an interesting challenge. My clients wanted to be able to seat a large number of people but also have a space that would feel more intimate. My solution was to divide the room in half visually with two pairs of Corinthian columns, and between the columns I installed a screen that follows a channel camouflaged by beams. When the screen closes, the table's size is reduced to sit eight rather than sixteen, but at full length it creates an elegant symmetry that gracefully fills the space. The chandeliers are also rigged to move on a track, to follow the table.

In the paneled library, another problem: The craftsmanship is impeccable, but the material is pine, inappropriate for a sophisticated Manhattan dwelling. So I commissioned an artisan to do a faux-bois treatment that resembles cherry. A state-of-the-art entertainment system blends seamlessly with the old-world atmosphere. And in a room with scant natural light, I placed a table by the one window for cozy dinners à deux.

Previous page: A nineteenth-century English gentleman's dressing table, in the vestibule to the master bathroom. *Right:* A Giacometti bust commands attention in the foyer, subtly counterbalanced by a nineteenth-century English mahogany demi-lune console, accentuated with a Henry Moore, and a nineteenth-century mirror in Dutch style.

The custom carpet in the library was woven in France, inspired by one in the Duke and Duchess of Windsor's house in the Bois de Boulogne. The paneling was given a faux bois finish to resemble cherry. A Chinese-inspired coffee table resides between sofas of my design. On the wall, a painting by Modigliani (1917).

Golds and ivories infuse the living room with a subtle glow. A pair of late-Georgian gilt-frame armchairs, an eighteenth-century English ottoman with gilt legs, sofas and armchairs of my design, a painting by Chagall—all help to inspire a feeling of understated luxury.

View into the library, with another Giacometti sculpture in the foreground echoing a painting by Jean Dubuffet on the library wall.

Maple cabinetry of my design enlivens the study, while a nineteenth-century English mahogany desk adds a layer of dignified elegance.

A study in understated grandeur. The early-nineteenth-century Swedish gilt-frame dining chairs upholstered in silk are identical to those in a suite in the Royal Palace in Stockholm. Eighteenth-century gilt pedestals flank a late Georgian mahogany breakfront. A pair of nineteenth-century bronze urns from the Rothschild collection complete the setting. Sculpture in niche by Aristide Maillol.

In the master bedroom, a Matisse painting sets the mood. Eighteenth-century Italian inlaid commodes support a pair of carved gilt lamps from Nancy Corzine. A small Diego Giacometti table in front of the window and a bench of my design reflect the painting's delicacy.

ACKNOWLEDGMENTS

There have been many people throughout my life who have played a role, both large and small, in helping me to make this glorious monograph a reality. I would like to offer a special thanks to:

Paige Rense, for her encouragement throughout my thirty years in the business; Paige has a special place in my heart.

Cynthia Conigliaro, for being my first contact with The Monacelli Press.

Urban O. Karlsson, for his endless devotion over the last ten years, both professionally and personally; for being my loyal partner and companion.

Anthony S. Mercante, for encouraging me to go into the field of design.

My mother, father, and sister, for supporting my dreams and creative tugs from very early in my life, beginning with encouraging me to learn the process of painting.

My amazing design team—Shaler Ladd III, Carlos A. Gonzalez, Dawn Zertuche, Sarah Peterson, Sara Ann Rolfes, Paulette Pascarella, Annaliese Pew, and Elizabeth Strianese; and a special thanks to Shaler for being with me for so long.

Manuel Tan, for translating my dreams into impeccable drawings.

Elizabeth Gaynor, for interpreting my dreams through the words in this book.

Takaaki Matsumoto and Amy Wilkins, for immediately understanding how to capture the purity of my work through the design of this book.

Karen Lehrman Bloch at Grafia Books, for ensuring that the words in this book reflect the elegance of the images, and for shepherding this project to its exquisite completion.

Andrea Monfried and Elizabeth White at Monacelli, for maintaining the high standards necessary to make this book such an extraordinary work of art.

My incredible clients, without them none of this would have been possible.

Margaret Dunne, James Huntington, Jeffrey Nemroff, and the rest of the *Architectural Digest* team for their unwavering support and professionalism.

Margaret Russell and Cindy Allen, for championing my work through the years, and for understanding how my projects could best be presented in graphic format.

Monica Geran, for being the first to discover my work and publish it in a magazine.

The gallerists who carry the beautiful items that make my projects come alive—Barry Friedman, Carole Hochman, Tony De Lorenzo, Adriana Friedman, Liz O'Brien, Mindy Papp, Regina Nuessle, Deborah Buck, Jean-Jacques and Agnes Dutko, Eric Allart, Paul and Carina Jackson, Alexandre Biaggi, Galerie Vallois, Jacques Lacoste, the late Annsofie Duval, Galerie Camoin, Roger Prigent and Yvonne Lacks of Malmaison, and Rozen Le Nagard.

The vendors who intuitively understand the essence of quality—Joe Lawrence, Lana Lawrence, John and Andrea Stark, Rick Zolt, and Audrie Smolen.

The artists who have created exquisite points of departure for my own work and for providing my projects with such a profound sensuality and soul—most especially, Manolo Valdés, Fernando Botero, Xavier Mascaró, and Eva Hild.

John King, who helped to create the wonderful garden in Garrison.

Finally, I would like to offer a special thanks to the paperboy who delivers *The New York Post* to me every morning, for helping me to start my day with good humor.